THE
POPPY

Published by IWM, Lambeth Road, London SE1 6HZ
iwm.org.uk

ISBN 978-1-912423-95-8

A catalogue record for this book is available from the British Library.

Printed and bound by Gomer

Colour reproduction by DL Imaging

Every effort has been made to contact all copyright holders. The
publishers will be glad to make good in future editions any error or
omissions brought to their attention.

EU Authorised Representative: EAS Europe – Mustamäe tee 50, 10621
Tallinn, Estonia, gpsr.requests@easproject.com

Front cover: 584538280 © Mandy Disher Photography / Getty Images

www.carbonbalancedprint.com
CBP2275

THE
POPPY

A Symbol of Remembrance

Laura Clouting

TABLE OF CONTENTS

THE
POPPY

✺ For Britain, the human cost of the First World War has never been surpassed. The years 1914 to 1918 saw its worst loss of life in a war. Three-quarters of a million servicemen died as a result of the conflict. When combined with the deaths from Britain's Empire forces, the death toll grew nearer to one million lives. The death count also included thousands of women who were killed while volunteering, often as nurses or for female branches of the armed services. Although the death toll once again ran into the hundreds of thousands, British losses in the Second World War were considerably fewer. One quarter of a million servicemen died in that war. Civilian casualties were far greater, though, with some 60,000 people killed in German air raids on Britain. The First World War's human impact extended to the wounded and those who became mentally ill as a result of their war service. The effects on their bodies and psyches were sometimes severe and permanent, never allowing the experience of war to be forgotten. Even those who returned home apparently unscathed were survivors of a seismic event.

With so many dead, British rituals of remembrance came to reflect the sheer enormity of this 'total war'. The conflict's scale had been shown in its tremendous demand for men, munitions and money, its political upheavals, the interdependence of the home and fighting fronts, the threat to national survival and the escalating human cost. From mantelpiece memorials to state-sponsored monuments, an industry of remembrance iconography revealed itself in hundreds of thousands of homes and within the civic fabric of Britain itself. One symbol came to embody the collective mourning and memory more powerfully than any other: the poppy.

The red poppy has arguably become the most enduring icon of remembrance – an instantly recognisable symbol of war's grave human cost. That it became so was the result of a botanical phenomenon during the First World War – the shocking burst of colourful plant life in otherwise unrelentingly bleak landscapes on the war's Western Front.

Overleaf Australian troops walk along a duckboard track through the remains of Chateau Wood, Third Battle of Ypres (Passchendaele), 29 October 1917.

Modern weaponry pulverised the earth, as well as bodies and buildings, in unprecedented waves of destruction. Yet the high-explosive shells that tore into the soil had a surprising generative effect. Inadvertently they created the perfect conditions in which a simple, translucent red flower could grow – *Papaver Rhoeas* – the red corn poppy.

The savage violence stirred the ground so effectively that millions of tall, slender poppy stalks flourished on the Western Front. Though it appeared so delicate and incongruous, this short-lived, crimson wildflower, which could reach over 75 cm (30 inches) in height, was actually rather robust. The annual plant thrived in fertile, well-drained soils such as chalk, which were a feature of the Somme battlefield in 1916. As the summer sun beat down, the poppies put on an expansive and extravagant display.

During the war, many soldiers plucked and pressed the fragile heads of the corn poppy into letters home as a botanical greeting. The petals gave a cheerful flash of colour in a drab world of khaki and mud. Other flowers also grew in parts of the Western Front, their beauty relished by soldiers otherwise surrounded by landscapes of devastation. Reginald Bryan recalled his delight at encountering wildflowers in springtime:

One afternoon at the end of April I went to a wood which had been destroyed by guns and had the surprise of my life. The trees had without exception been splintered to smithereens and the ground was strewed with wreckage and broken branches, but I also found that the wood was covered with a mass of yellow wildflowers, oxslips and cowslips! Elsewhere there was not a sign of a flower but here they were growing in thousands. I was delighted with my find and gathered some and sent a box of them home to Mother.

Yet it was the poppy that captured the imagination of contemporaries to become the most evocative symbol of the war.

Overleaf *The Cemetery, Etaples, 1919* by official war artist Sir John Lavery. The painting shows women tending to graves during the cemetery's earliest days, before the erection of formal headstones.

'IN

FLANDERS
FIELDS'

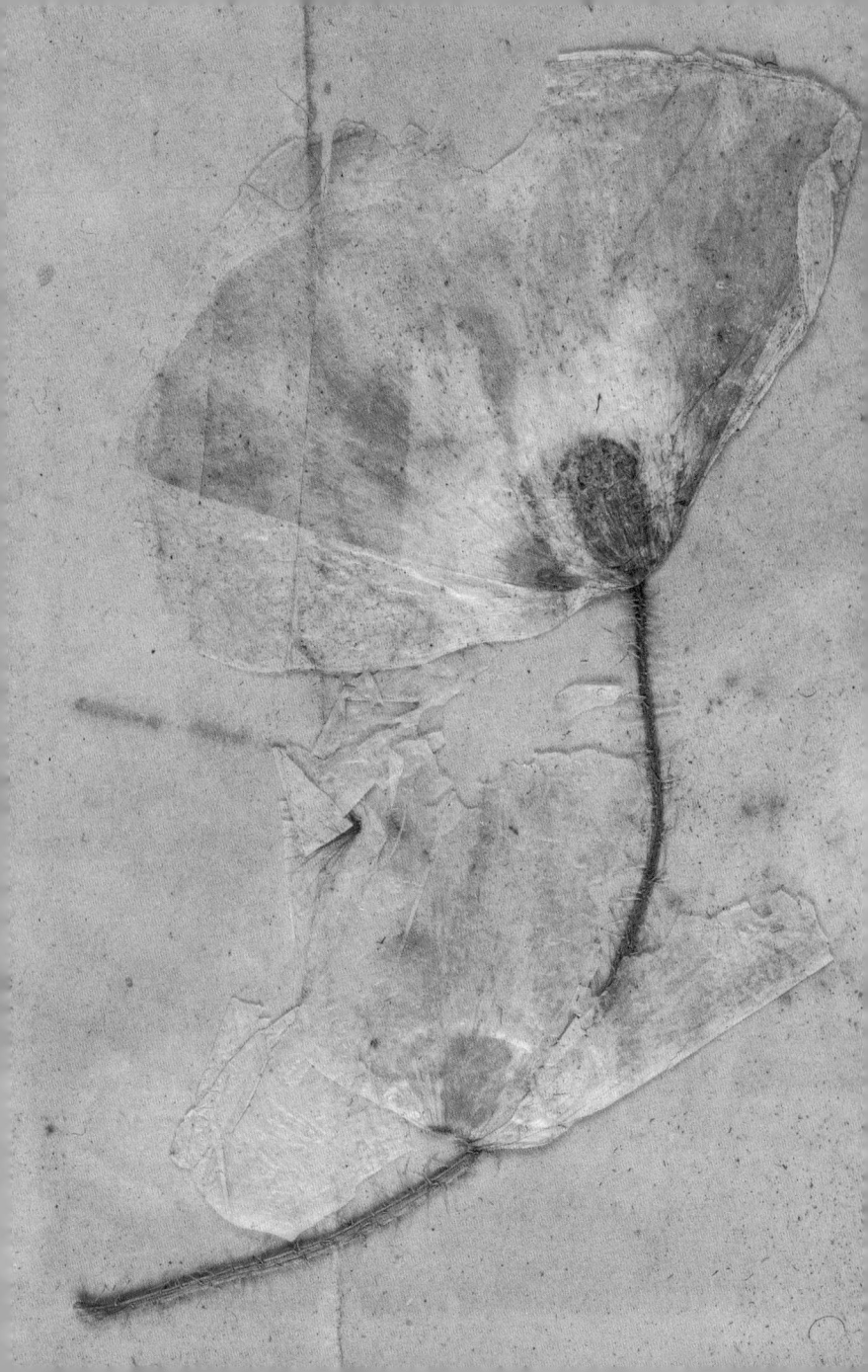

✳ One of the war's most famous poems about the flower had its roots in the bloody spring of 1915, as the war entered a grinding deadlock. The Second Battle of Ypres was one of many failed attempts to break the stalemate. Canadian physician Lieutenant Colonel John McCrae worked in a dressing station extremely close to the front line; here, embedded with the military, he could quickly tend to wounds sustained in the fighting. McCrae was no stranger to the battlefield. He had fought in the Boer Wars in South Africa at the turn of the century before returning across the Atlantic, very much by choice, to serve in the forces of the British Empire once more.

Like most of the soldier poets who became famous after the war, McCrae was not an established writer. He had poems published in his university newspaper in Montreal, but poetry was no more than a pastime. As a military doctor, he used snatched moments to pen verse in response to what he experienced and witnessed on active service, as did other soldier poets. Like millions

Opposite A poppy picked from the trenches during the Third Battle of Ypres by George Palmer of the Machine Gun Corps.
Overleaf A poppy from the Western Front, picked by Joseph Shaddick during his war service and sent home to his wife. This example was subsequently framed, along with an Army Field Service Postcard, one of the simplest ways for a soldier to send a brief update home. Many families received similar poppy mementoes.

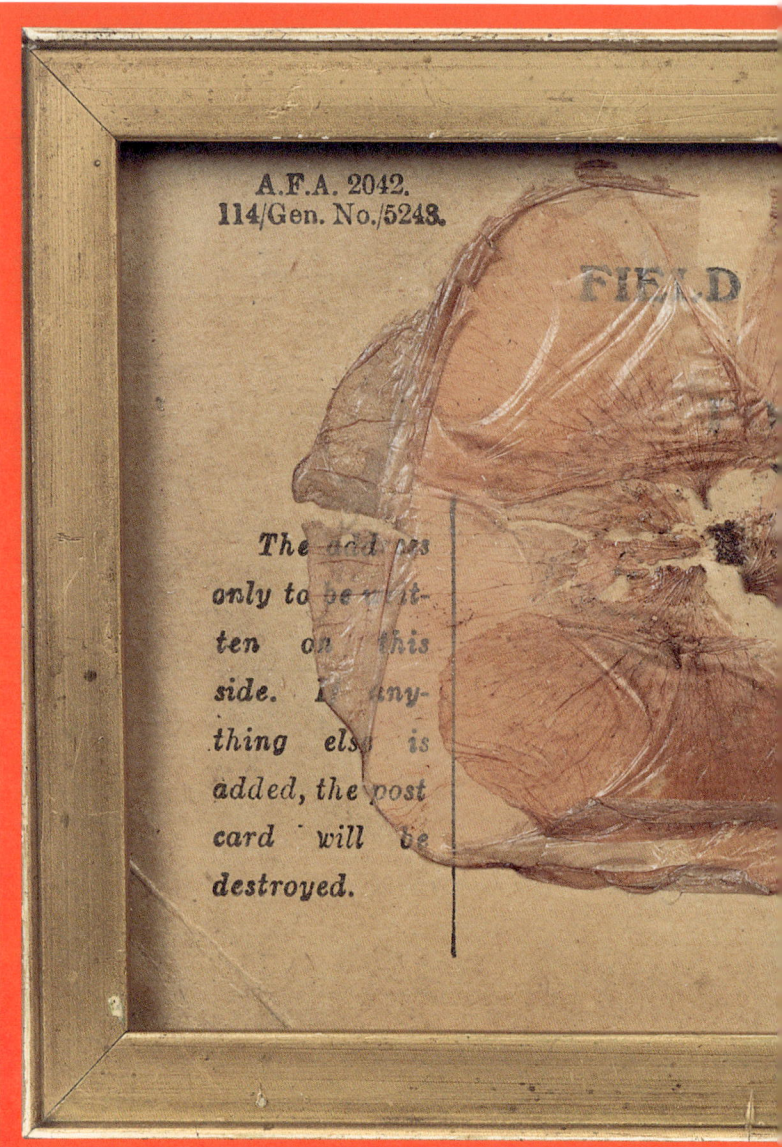

A.F.A. 2042.
114/Gen. No./5248.

FIELD

The add*ess
only to *e *it-
ten on this
side. I* any-
thing els* is
added, the post
card will be
destroyed.

"If ye break faith —
we shall not sleep"

BUY VICTO

RY BONDS

more, McCrae also corresponded with home. In a letter to his mother written during the Second Battle of Ypres in late April 1915, the 42-year-old described the scene around him:

Traffic whizzed by – ambulances, transport, ammunition, supplies, despatch riders – and the shells thundered into the town, or burst high in the air nearer us, and the refugees streamed. Women, old men, little children, hopeless, tearful, quiet or excited, tired, dodging the traffic, – and the wounded in singles or in groups. Here and there I could give a momentary help, and the ambulances picked up as they could. So the cold moonlight night wore on – no change save that the towers of Ypres showed up against the glare of the city burning; and the shells still sailed in.

Early in May 1915, in a break from tending to the wounded and dying, McCrae wrote a new poem. The

Previous page The title of this First World War poster was inspired by the concluding lines of McCrae's poem, 'In Flanders Fields'.
Opposite Lieutenant-Colonel John McCrae became one of the most famous soldier poets thanks to his tribute to the war dead, 'In Flanders Fields'. The poem explicitly linked remembrance of the war dead to the corn poppies that flourished near graves on the Western Front.

CAPTAIN GILBERT TYNDALE-LEA, M. C.
1654 SHATTO STREET.
LOS ANGELES, CALIFORNIA, U. S. A.

TELEPHONE
DREXEL 3610

In Flanders Fields

In Flanders fields the poppies grow
Between the crosses, row on row,
That mark our place : and in the sky,
The larks still bravely singing, fly,
Scarce heard amid the guns below.

We are the dead. Short days ago
We lived, felt dawn, saw sunset glow,
Loved, and were loved, and now we lie
In Flanders fields.

Take up our quarrel with the foe.
To you from failing hands we throw
The torch : be yours to hold it high !
If ye break faith with us who die
We shall not sleep, though poppies grow
In Flanders fields.

John McCrae

Above is a tracing of an original copy, written for and given to me
by Major John McCrae, on the day he wrote his famous poem, April 29th
1915.

Above A tracing of an original holograph copy of John McCrae's poem 'In Flanders Fields'. It was given to Captain Gilbert Tyndale-Lea by McCrae on 29 April 1915 – the day he wrote the poem during a break from treating the wounded.

poppies that grew in abundance in the expanding 'Essex Farm' cemetery nearby were his inspiration. The poem, most commonly known as 'In Flanders Fields', was written in the aftermath of the death of a close friend in action. Its very first iteration read:

In Flanders fields the poppies grow
Between the crosses, row on row,
That mark our place: and in the sky
The larks, still bravely singing, fly
Scarce heard amid the guns below.

We are the dead. Short days ago
We lived, felt dawn, saw sunset glow,
Loved and were loved, and now we lie
In Flanders fields.

Take up our quarrel with the foe;
To you from failing hands we throw
The torch; be yours to hold it high,
If ye break faith with us who die
We shall not sleep, though poppies grow
In Flanders fields.

A later tweak saw the word 'grow' in the first line become 'blow'. For some the poem served as a hopeful beacon of life in the midst of death; conversely its colour reminded others of a brutal blood sacrifice. McCrae himself associated the profligate wildflowers with the spiralling tally of war dead. Whatever people saw in the poppy, it almost always went beyond its botanical status as a rampant weed.

McCrae did not keep his poem private. Later in the year he sent the piece off to *Punch*, a hugely popular satirical magazine, and the verses first appeared in print on 8 December 1915. McCrae's work seized the imagination of soldiers and civilians alike. In a contextual essay about McCrae's life, written to accompany an edition of his poetry printed in 1919, his friend Sir Andrew Macphail described the widespread affection for the poem:

Overleaf Edwin Martin's *The 42nd Casualty Clearing Station, Douai, 1919* shows the numerous white tents of a casualty clearing station in the French countryside during the First World War. In the foreground is a road, with a few trees on the left and some poppies among the long grass.

It circulates, as a song should circulate, by the living word of mouth, not by printed characters. That is the true test of poetry – its insistence on making itself learnt by heart.

McCrae's war experiences did not end there, although he never worked so close to the frontline after 1915. He had senior postings in a major military hospital behind the lines near Boulogne in France. The strain weakened him, according to Macphail, and he died from the rapid onset of double pneumonia and cerebral infection in January 1918:

After his experience at the front the old gaiety never returned. There were moments of irascibility and moods of irritation. The desire for solitude grew upon him, and with Bonfire and Bonneau [McCrae's dogs] he would go apart for long afternoons far afield by the roads and lanes about Boulogne. The truth is: he felt that he and all had failed, and that the torch was thrown from failing hands. We have heard much of the suffering, the misery, the cold, the wet, the gloom of those first three winters; but no tongue has yet uttered the inner misery of heart that was bred of those three years of failure to break the enemy's force.

Opposite A British soldier stands besides the grave of a comrade near Pilckem during the Third Battle of Ypres, 22nd August 1917.

KEEPING
THE FAITH

✹ John McCrae never lived to see the full impact of his poem on the flower it took its inspiration from. The poppy's status as the foremost symbol of remembrance and a fundraising icon began after his lifetime. Two days before the First World War ended, a 49-year-old American academic from the University of Georgia stumbled across a reprinting of McCrae's poem. Moina Michael had left a teaching post to work for the Young Women's Christian Association (YWCA) Overseas War Secretaries (OWS). While at work in New York City on 9 November 1918, a reprint of McCrae's poem in the *Ladies' Home Journal* caught her attention.

In her memoir, Michael described reading the poem and her response as a 'full spiritual experience'. She penned her own poem in direct response to McCrae's lines. Her creation, 'We Shall Keep the Faith', read:

Previous page Wreaths being assembled by employees of the British Legion Poppy Factory at Richmond. Disabled veterans were recruited as workers in the factory and its Scottish equivalent in Edinburgh.

Oh! You who sleep in Flanders' fields,
Sleep sweet – to rise anew,
We caught the torch you threw,
And holding high we kept
The faith with those who died.
We cherish too, the poppy red
That grows on fields where valor led.
It seems to signal to the skies
That blood of heroes never dies,
But lends a lustre to the red
Of the flower that blooms above the dead
In Flanders' fields.
And now the torch and poppy red
Wear in honour of our dead.
Fear not that ye have died for naught
We've learned the lesson that ye taught
In Flanders' fields.

For Moina Michael the poppy was a symbolic link between the living and the dead. Two days later she decided to make the link tangible. Armed with cash donated by YMCA conference delegates, she purchased 25 artificial flowers in a nearby department store on 11 November 1918. On Michael's return, attendees of the conference enthusiastically pinned the flowers to their lapels. With the fighting having just ended with a ceasefire that same day, the symbolic power of the poppy gained traction.

Although her efforts were beset by difficulties, Moina Michael fervently advocated the wearing of the poppy far and wide. In 1920 the American Legion, a major veterans' organisation, formally approved the poppy as its symbol for remembering the war dead. All funds raised through the distribution of artificial flowers would be channelled for the aid of wounded veterans. Later the Legion embraced the daisy as its symbol, before reinstating the poppy. Its initial embrace of the red flower was instrumental in the poppy's transatlantic success.

Previous page Poppies were sold during the Second World War as a symbol of remembrance, continuing the tradition begun after the First World War. Here, poppies are sold to troops, 11 November 1945.

The poppy might never have made its way to Britain were it not for the efforts of another woman present at the YMCA conference in November 1918. Anna Guérin, a YMCA secretary from war-ravaged France, spearheaded a campaign for the red poppy to become a remembrance symbol in her homeland. Already well-known as the 'Poppy Lady of France', Guérin believed that the red memorial bloom should be adopted on a wider scale. She organised a network of French war widows to make poppy flowers from silk. Guérin arranged for these to be sold and distributed to global organisations, including the American Legion, to raise funds for their causes – namely veterans with disabilities or those in financial hardship. Guérin's charity for war-orphaned children, La Ligue Américaine Française des Enfants, would in turn benefit from a share of the funds raised through the sale of poppies.

THE
POWER
OF THE
POPPY

✸ Britain became the focus of Guérin's next campaign. She arrived in August 1921, bringing her vehement energy to the door of the newly formed British Legion. The organisation was a conglomeration of veterans' associations with a fundraising arm; it had the personal patronage of Earl Douglas Haig, Britain's most senior commander during the war. The idea for the red poppy as a remembrance symbol and fundraising spur moved him greatly and he personally endorsed the campaign. Haig's reputation was in its zenith, despite the enormous loss of life that occurred under his command and which was to bring his reputation into question in later reappraisals of his career. In the 1920s it was widely perceived that Haig's leadership had contributed to the Allied victory over Germany. His support was considered a great asset to the early poppy appeals.

Opposite Field Marshal Sir Douglas Haig, who commanded the British Expeditionary Force in France and Belgium from December 1915 until the end of the war. Haig's legacy has been hotly contested in recent years, notably regarding his rationale for the campaigns in which hundreds of thousands of British soldiers under his command died. In the 1920s Haig devoted himself to the care of ex-servicemen in need and lent his name to the fundraising of voluntary donations through the sale of artificial poppies.

Guérin persuaded the British Legion to order a vast tranche of the silk poppies made by French war widows, with a percentage of the funds raised to be set aside for her own work in France. The Legion needed to raise essential funds for its own ambitions to support British veterans in peacetime so – despite reservations about whether the idea would catch on – 9 million poppies were ordered. The first Poppy Day was held on 11 November 1921. The British Legion decided to align its fundraising efforts with Armistice Day, which had already become a firm fixture of significance in the national calendar.

Volunteers were rallied across the country – a huge logistical effort. Each wore a tray full of the silk flowers to sell in the streets and public areas. People were asked to make a donation of whatever they could afford in return for a poppy, at no fixed price. The power of the appeal was glaringly obvious from the start; sellers could not keep up with demand. It was a runaway success, raising the equivalent of over 4 million pounds.

The French silk flowers were handed over, along with a leaflet containing both Canadian John McCrae's poem and American Moina Michael's response to it, drawing together all of the threads that had brought the poppy to British shores. The flower became deeply associated with the loss of life in the war as much as helping those who had survived it at personal cost.

Given this triumph, in order to ensure an adequate and ambitious supply of poppies and to direct all donations to British veterans, the British Legion made the decision to abandon Anna Guérin's silk poppies in future appeals. Instead, it set up a bespoke artificial poppy factory to provide employment directly to wounded ex-servicemen. This was the brainchild of Major George Howson. There were concerns that Britain should be fundraising for its own veterans as a priority, whatever the humanitarian needs in former Allied countries.

Demand in England was so high in the early appeals that Scotland was not adequately supplied with remembrance poppies, despite the country having suffered in the region of 100,000 deaths attributable to the war, both during the conflict and in the years after it. Earl Haig's connections with Scotland were also plentiful; he was born in Edinburgh and

Overleaf A British artificial fabric poppy from an early Poppy Appeal. A tag attached to the poppy bears the inscription 'EARL HAIG'S APPEAL For Ex-Service Men of all Ranks and their Dependents BRITISH LEGION REMEMBRANCE DAY'.

EARL HAIG'S APPEAL
For Ex-Service Men of all
Ranks and their Defendents.

buried in the Scottish Borders following his death in 1928. His wife Dorothy fronted a push to set up an exclusive production line for Scotland. The Lady Haig Poppy Factory was established in Edinburgh in 1926 to do just that. The poppies sold north of the border differed by having four red leaves and no green leaf – something still attributed today as being 'botanically incorrect'. Britain's poppy factories soon branched out, as the flowers were incorporated into the ceremonial aspects of Armistice Day formalities. Wreaths were produced for individuals and veterans' associations to place a more substantial floral tribute on war graves, at local war memorials or upon major sites such as the Cenotaph.

Volunteer poppy sellers were integral to the success of the appeals. This was recognised by Earl Haig in his lifetime. In a widely reproduced letter of thanks, he warmly acknowledged the army of sellers:

As the Poppy symbolises the
sacrifice of those who laid down
their lives, so your kindly help for
those gallant survivors who are
now in want, typifies that spirit
of gratitude and service, which is
beyond all praise or earthly reward.

POPPIES OF

PEACE

AND WAR

✿ Whether John McCrae could ever have imagined the connection between his poem's poppies and the status they would acquire in Britain as the foremost symbol of the war in which he died is impossible to gauge. The tradition of wearing poppies allowed an individual tribute to become part of a collective movement to ensure the First World War's human cost was remembered. Artificial poppies continue to be sold in Britain and parts of its former Empire to raise money for service personnel, veterans and their dependents in need, and to remember those who lost their lives in the First World War and subsequent conflicts.

But the poppy and the politics around it have become complex in more recent times, especially as new conflicts have arisen without the widespread societal backing witnessed during the world wars. The red poppy has been subject to both rejection and appropriation, and its meaning contested. As early as the 1920s the matter of other groups selling 'competing' red poppies had also become a concern.

Opposite A lapel badge worn by members of the British Legion, which was formed in 1920 from an amalgamation of three ex-servicemen's organisations: the Comrades of the Great War, the National Association of Discharged Sailors and Soldiers and the National Federation of Discharged and Demobilised Sailors and Soldiers. The organisation became known as the Royal British Legion in 1971.

Brighton MP Sir Cooper Rawson pushed for a law preventing the import and sale of German-manufactured red poppies that had been making their way into Britain in 1928. He considered moral outrage the appropriate response towards anyone guilty of producing 'rival' poppies in Britain itself, deceitfully diverting funds from the British Legion's work:

Unfortunately, there are in this country at the present time, I am ashamed to say, people who are manufacturing, for profit, British Legion poppies in competition with the British Legion official poppy. These are being manufactured, distributed, and sold merely to undercut the British Legion official poppy. ... I think we shall have to leave it to the discerning British public to find them out and when they have found them out to expose them.

Opposite Poppy wreaths are laid at the base of the Cenotaph in London during the interwar period. Artificial poppies ranged from the simple lapel variant to elaborate wreaths laid by veterans' associations or senior royal, political and military figures at remembrance services. Today the Royal British Legion's fundraising poppy range includes jewellery and clothing.

Above A white poppy sold by the Peace Pledge Union in the 1930s. These alternative artificial poppies symbolised opposition to war: the word 'PEACE' is embossed in the centre. Like early British Legion red poppies, this white poppy is made from fabric.

Alternative poppies reflect diverging attitudes. White poppies were, and remain, the most familiar alternative poppy. They were first sold by the social justice movement the Co-operative Women's Guild in 1933, with the Peace Pledge Union (PPU) taking over in 1934. The white poppy's meaning was stridently anti-war. The wearing of a PPU flower had three main aims: to remember all the victims of war, both military and civilian, to stand up for peace and to challenge militarism, reflecting the belief that 'working for peace is the natural consequence of remembering the victims of war'.

The present day (now Royal) British Legion regards its red poppies as 'a symbol of both Remembrance and hope for a peaceful future'. The act of wearing a poppy remains deeply personal. As the Royal British Legion has stated:

Previous page A field of poppies near Eye, Suffolk, during the Second World War.
Overleaf Wing Commander Guy Gibson VC, who won a Victoria Cross for leading the Dambusters Raid, sitting in a poppy field reading a book at RAF Scampton, 22 July 1943. The poppy retained its significance during the Second World War as a symbol of remembrance.

Wearing a poppy is still a very personal choice, reflecting individual experiences and personal memories. It is never compulsory but is greatly appreciated by those who it is intended to support.

Popular culture has been highly influential in shaping impressions of the First World War in the years since the conflict ended. Art, poems, literature, stage productions, feature films, television and music have told stories – real and imagined – about the conflict's brutal violence while cultivating empathy for the First World War's human cost. The symbolic red poppy is often a feature of creative works, interwoven through imaginative portrayals of the battlefield featuring the crimson wildflower.

In 2014, at the centenary of the First World War's outbreak, a major art installation harnessed the red poppy on an epic scale. The installation *Blood Swept Lands and Seas of Red* was the work of artist Paul Cummins and designer Tom Piper. A collaboration with Historic Royal Palaces, the Tower of London became the temporary home to 888,246 hand-crafted ceramic poppies, planted by an army of volunteers. Each poppy was handcrafted from clay. Each represented the life of a serviceman from the forces of Britain and its Empire during the war. The artwork was installed at the Tower between August and November.

The planted poppies slowly but surely grew in number until the final flower was planted on 11 November 2014 as part of remembrance rituals associated with the date of the ceasefire on the Western Front in 1918.

The sea of poppies was joined by two dramatic sculptural elements, *Weeping Window* and the *Wave*. The former gave the impression of poppies pouring from a high window down to the ground, while the latter formed an arch around the Tower's entrance. The seismic work was intended to convey the sheer scale of loss suffered in the name of Britain's First World War effort. It became a sensation. The installation was caught the public imagination to an extraordinary extent. An estimated 5 million people visited the Tower of London to catch a glimpse of the spectacle as it developed.

Blood Swept Lands and Seas of Red was only ever intended to be temporary. Come the end of the year, the ocean of poppies had been gradually removed. The ceramic flowers were offered for individual sale to raise money for selected veterans' charities. Though originally intended as a temporary installation, it was agreed that elements of the artwork should be preserved for the nation.

Wave and *Weeping Window* were toured around the UK from 2014 until 2018. People had the chance to experience the visual and emotional impact of the

Overleaf The *Blood Swept Lands and Seas of Red* installation at the Tower of London in 2014.

ceramic poppies for themselves in locations from Liverpool to Orkney. The four-year tour allowed for reflection on people's personal links to the First World War and to participate in a shared experience.

One hundred years on from the end of the 'war to end all wars', the major structural elements were reconfigured into the artwork, *Poppies*. This impressive piece was made from 12,960 handcrafted poppies and went on permanent display at IWM North in 2021. It joined the museum's vast archive of artworks, objects, letters, diaries, film and photographs which form a lasting record of the ways people – both civilian and military – have been affected by war and conflict.

In 2021, *Poppies* was installed for permanent public display at Manchester's IWM North. Designed by world-renowned architect Daniel Libeskind to represent a globe shattered by conflict, the museum is now home to the ceramic flowers which cascade 30 metres down the unique architecture of its Air Shard before pooling at the bottom.

Visitors are encouraged to engage with *Poppies* as both an important piece of social history as well as a conduit for reflection on war's human impact.

It is clear that cultural creations have become a way of connecting with war's human cost. From best-selling literature to award-winning popular films, the First World War has been imaginatively conceived by writers, poets, filmmakers, musicians and artists over the decades. Some of this material was created by people who had personally experienced the very action their works portrayed. More recent works have been inspired by events long after their conclusion.

Amidst this outpouring of cultural interpretations, the red poppy remains the most potent symbol of the First World War's human cost. It has become synonymous with the devastating numbers of lives lost during this momentous conflict. Engagement with the annual Poppy Appeal to raise funds for service personnel, veterans and their families continues. The poppy, with its symbolic roots arising from John McCrae's memorable poem, has provided a means for later generations to consider the causes, course and consequences of war and its profound impact on people's lives.

Overleaf The *Poppies* on display at IWM North. *Poppies: Wave and Weeping Window* were purchased for the nation by The Clore Duffield Foundation and Lady Susie Sainsbury's Backstage Trust in 2014 and went on permanent display at IWM North in 2021.